Doors of the W

Other books by Jean-Philippe and Dominique Lenclos:
Colors of the World
Windows of the World
Couleurs de la France
Couleurs de l'Europe

Doors of the World

Jean-Philippe and Dominique Lenclos

Foreword by Tom Porter

W. W. Norton & Company

New York • London

To Jean Widmer

Copyright © 2001 by Groupe Moniteur (Editions du Moniteur), Paris
English translation copyright © 2005 by W. W. Norton & Company, Inc.

Originally published in French as PORTES DU MONDE

All rights reserved
Printed in Italy

For information about permission to reproduce selections from this book,
write to Permissions, W. W. Norton & Company, Inc., 500 Fifth Avenue,
New York, NY 10110

Translation by Andrea Costella
Manufacturing by Rotolito Lombarda
Book design by Philippe Millot
Production manager: Leeann Graham

Library of Congress Cataloging-in-Publication Data

Lenclos, Jean-Philippe.
    [Portes du monde. English]
    Doors of the world / Jean-Philippe and Dominique Lenclos.
       p.   cm.
    ISBN 0-393-73187-1 (pbk.)
    1. Doorways. I. Lenclos, Dominique. II. Title.

    NA3010 .L4613 2005
    721'.822—dc22   2005047307

W. W. Norton & Company, Inc., 500 Fifth Avenue, New York, N.Y. 10110
www.wwnorton.com
W. W. Norton & Company Ltd., Castle House, 75/76 Wells St.,
London W1T 3QT

0 9 8 7 6 5 4 3 2 1

Foreword

I first encountered the color research of Jean-Philippe and Dominique Lenclos at the "France is Color" exhibit at London's Design Centre in 1974. The focal point of the exhibit was a large matrix of rich pigments that turned out to be soil samples taken from the diverse geological and climatic regions of their native France. Their work was documented in a trilogy of ensuing books culminating in *Colors of the World* (Norton, 2004), which explains the Lenclos's approach to environmental color—that is, that the diversity of color signifies, in the words of the late Charles Moore, the all-important "sense of place."

Their fourth book, *Doors of the World*, has to be regarded in this context. Emerging as it does from their well-documented investigations into architectural color, this book—the companion volume to which is *Windows of the World*—completes their study of a key feature of any habitat's facade. The Lenclos's study results from a research program that is both simple and logical. First, selecting sites typical of a region and armed with the knowledge that traditional settlements are built from the substrate upon which they stand, they take color samples of locally applied pigment from each architectural component of a habitat, in addition to its building materials and the structure's indigenous flora and local geology. Later, back in their studio, the samples are meticulously color matched in gouache and assembled into color palettes, which are classified to represent facades and architectural details. The resulting palettes then function as a design tool, able to be applied to both existing and proposed architecture. Initially, the Lenclos's research led to a series of commissions in which they were asked to provide color maps for various developing French towns, including Creteuil and Cergy-Pontoise, as well as for countless traditional settlements across France. Later, enthusiastically adopted by the Japanese Color Planning Center in Tokyo, the Lenclos turned their attention to a broader, more international spectrum, establishing themselves as the leading colorists of Europe, if not the world.

As part of their investigation into the color of architecture, the door represents that part of a fenestration which, more than any other, symbolizes the architectural badge of occupancy or ownership. Indeed, like cosmetics, clothing, or even the color of our automobile, the color of the door represents yet another layer of meaning in the projection of our personality onto the outside world. For example, door colors say much about the psychology of those who reside within; they can shout or whisper, be welcoming or forbidding, amplify or downplay status. Above all, they are an architectural element that embodies deep social and emotional significance. Doors are a threshold, a transitional zone that marks the passage between the exterior and interior domain, between public and private. The greater the desire for physical or psychological separation between inside and outside worlds, generally the more elaborate and protracted the threshold transition. According to Martin Heidegger, the twentieth-century German philosopher, the door is the point at the beginning of a dwelling. It marks a habitat in the most basic sense because it is a highly defined location. A directional bias is often associated with this zone, namely that of moving from a less bounded to a more contained space, and is accompanied by the idea of entering. Accordingly, from the earliest human settlements to the present, ritual and specific modes of behavior and body language have come to be associated with the process of opening a door and crossing its threshold: removing shoes or hat, paying respect to the protecting deities, exchanging greetings with the host, and, more recently, submitting to security checks.

As this book so beautifully illustrates, the physical form and appearance of the door vary widely depending on the cultural setting.

With few exceptions, it is clearly defined and its conventions are well understood within a culture. In *Doors of the World* we find this extreme variegation played out through the creativity of the structure itself, the elaboration of detail and ornament, and the contrast between the implied character of inside and outside space—all employed to emphasize the separation between home and the public world beyond.

Tom Porter

Preface

After three books dedicated to the color of vernacular habitats in France, Europe, and the rest of the world, it struck us as opportune to examine the major components of houses. This study looks at doors.

Indeed, architecture is essentially founded on the composition of functional elements such as doors, which give access to the interior of the house, and windows or other openings, which allow light to enter into a home and its inhabitants to watch, through them, what happens outside.

The door is steeped in mystery. It encloses, hides, and protects a space from foul weather and intruders, conversely, it can open to disclose what it hides, something somber, secret, unknown. The door, therefore, is a sort of passageway between two worlds, two states, between the unknown and the known, between public and private, between the profane and the sacred.

Unlike a temple, a house is not a means of access to any sort of revelation, but access to the intimate, the private, an idea which invites open doors.

This welcoming, this call of hospitality to passersby, is measured by how open the entryway is: ajar, half-open, open but protected by a curtain, or all the way open.

If you were to compare a house to a human face, the door is the mouth (in fact, in a number of African languages, the door is referred to as "the mouth of the house"); the windows, subject of a companion volume, are the eyes, protected by the eyelids—shutters or other coverings that open, open part way, or are closed.

We are interested in the elements that appeal to designers, architects, colorists, and, more generally, to everyone sensitive to architectural nuance, no matter how modest. Like our previous studies, this book purposely distances itself from the monumental, whether civil or religious architecture.

From the various countries we visited, we have selected aspects of certain openings that interest us: in some places, it is the design and proportions; in others, the particular character of the relationship between colors; in others still, the poetry conveyed when inhabitants embellish and personalize their entryways with climbing plants or carefully chosen curtains, for example. The style of a door is an equally important factor to consider because it expresses and reveals the architectural vocabulary of a given time.

The images we have selected seek to emphasize what is sometimes misunderstood, even mistaken, but basically too often ignored by inhabitants themselves—the harmony born from a balance of proportion, design, material, and color. The images do not constitute an exhaustive or theoretical study of doors.

The approach here is really the point of view of ordinary passersby attentive to the built environment. We gathered images from here and there according to significant elements and what would pique interest, admiration, or emotion. This collection is therefore personal and subjective.

This book is the result of an often difficult selection: too many doors find themselves in the way of pipes, electric cables, or unfortunate transformations effected by the inhabitant. Our photographs rarely assemble all the aspects of an ideal door, but offer an idea of the theme's rich variations. This infinite richness is testimony to the creative genius of architects, artisans, and inhabitants themselves, in a historic, geographic, and cultural context.

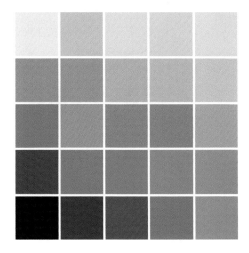

This ensemble of vignettes demonstrates in a simple fashion the colors of twenty-five houses from Bonnieux, in the Vaucluse region of France.

The various woodwork tonalities stand out against the sand-colored palette of the facades. The doors, especially, are of sober, refined sand, beige, ochre, and gray tints, to which are added shades of green, creating a distinctive, supporting palette.

Doors

Doors condition the existence of all habitats, no matter what kind, because a habitat is not a habitat without a door.

The principal door of a residence often carries a particular visual importance: it clearly marks the entry of the home, even when the facade is plain and bare—a small cornice, pediment, sculpted lintel, decorative ironwork, a door knocker, a large keyhole—all elegantly and discreetly underscoring and personalizing this passageway.

A passage from exterior to interior, or from interior to exterior, a passage over which the god Janus presides, separating the good and the bad spirits; an entryway, the "mouth of the home," is more or less welcoming, depending on its occupants and local customs. The land-scape painter Gilles Clément remarked that by "traveling, one can classify countries by the way in which their doors stand open, closed, or ajar—their state of wakefulness. The degree to which a residential door is open is a measure of how welcoming it is, and establishes a code shared among its people" (Clément Gilles, *Les Portes*, Paris, 1998).

Doors can not be separated from their surroundings, which determine the breadth of their opening. In a traditional country house, the frame, composed of a lintel, a doorjamb, and a doorstep, are generally works of artisans and demonstrate their true technical and artistic savoir-faire.

The lintel, whose function it is to support the weight of the wall above the door, is often formed from a single piece of wood or stone, as is the case in more modest residences. When entryways are larger, a triangular or arched panel softens the lintel while spreading the weight of the masonry above. The doorjambs are made of brick or stone cut to size.

Tradtionally, the lintel is the masonry element on which is inscribed the date of the house's construction, the name of the owner, other decorative formulas, or protective symbols that vary according to locale.

Moreover, lintels and doorjambs also offer opportunities for diverse ornamentation, where artisans can give free rein to their creativity.

As for doors themselves, composed of pivoting elements that allow for passage, outside the world of modern mass production, no two are exactly the same: form, proportion, design, material, and color are all components that vary according to locale, custom, ingenuity of the artisan, fancy of the inhabitant, and the mode of architecture employed.

Doors are usually rectangular in shape and tall enough to allow a person to stand in the frame. Until the appearance of modern building materials, the breadth of doors in traditional homes essentially depended on the length of the piece of wood or stone that was used as the lintel.

In rural areas—on a farm, for example—the basic form and proportion of the door is determined in equal parts by its use and function: a single door, a double-door that swings open to allow agricultural equipment to move through it, or a Dutch door in which the upper part can open like a window, while the lower one remains closed to prevent animals from entering the barn.

In urban or suburban households, a larger door, possibly with molded or sculpted panels, neatly signifies—by means of a cornice, a fanlight, or several doorsteps—the social status of the owner and the period of construction. This is particularly true of entryways in city homes whose ornaments and motifs are more refined than those in rural areas.

The proportions of a door are determined by architectural choices as well as by the dimensions of the facade and other openings. The placement of the door on the facade—central or off center—also gives a certain character to the habitat.

The question of door design is difficult to answer because, from the simplest assembly of planks to the most refined and elaborate woodwork, all design approaches are possible and worthy of study.

Door design is directly tied to its material composition and is also influenced by the specific artisanal traditions of its place.

Don't overlook the aesthetic contribution of functional metalwork by ironsmiths or other artisans, such as doorknobs, hinges, locks, and sometimes the door knocker. Even nails that give support to structural weak spots in wood form a geometric motif that can give a door its particular character.

Wood is the traditional construction material of doors. The assembly of planks results in an array of compositions, from simple to very complex. In some countries, other materials such as sheet metal, aluminum, or plastic coexist with wood or are gradually replacing it. In countries with warm climates, curtains are permanent components of a door when the door is open; made of cloth or dangling strings of rope, plastic, or wooden beads, curtains allow interior air circulation while offering protection from sun, flies, and the unwanted gaze of passersby.

The color of a door is a major component in the chromatic palette of the home, particularly at the main entrance; occupants look not only to protect their home from bad weather but also to reaffirm and differentiate their style and taste through color choice.

The color palette, however, is very much tied to regional customs. We were not surprised to find black doors in England and in the United States, a color hardly ever found in Latin countries.

Rural towns often display doors of natural wood with lovely gray tones, a patina acquired over time from the weather. These doors, often barn or pen doors, recall a time when protective paint was not used as a matter of course. The earliest paints came from mineral pigments, followed by lively, more saturated tones from organic-based pigments and, simultaneously, colorless varnish that allowed the natural grain of wood to show through while reinforcing its base color. More recently, we have stains that tint wood a transparent color.

This chart presents an inventory of colors taken from twenty-nine sites in France. A color synthesis chart, it illustrates the concept of the "geography of color," a system through we can characterize the habitats of every country and every region by a unique chromatic palette.

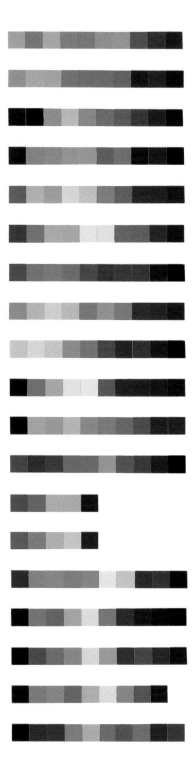

France

By covering the different regions of France and detailing the particularities of their habitats, canton by canton, village by village, it is easy to dwell on the typology and character of the architectural components that determine a region's distinctiveness.

Among these components, the entryway is undoubtedly the element that first attracts our gaze, not only because of its essential function—to allow access to the interior of a residence—but also because of the unique attention given to it by its owner, demonstrating a desire to make a home as beautiful and welcoming as possible. Classical architecture offers a number of examples of simple, almost austere facades with, for example, a lovely studded or molded paneled door that highlights a stone-framed doorway of varying size.

Here artisans can express themselves in all their glory and creative fantasy, as well as provide numerous examples of their work (particularly in smaller villages, where the workmanship of doors is simpler, a fact that does not detract from their beauty at all).

Doors are traditionally made of wood, often protected by varnish or paint; oak doors remaining in their natural color take on a beautiful gray patina over time. Sometimes the door is the same color as the shutters, which is often the case with homes on the coast of Brittany (we have noticed that the paint used by fishermen to coat the outside of their boats can also be found on the doors and shutters of their homes), and sometimes different: in the Vendée region, you might come across a walnut-stained door with green shutters; in the Dordogne, a green door with gray shutters.

If we were to define the most often used tonalities of doors in France, brown and wood-colored tones would dominate, followed by a palette of greens and grays, and, finally, ivory, white, and sand colors. Blue tends to be limited to maritime regions.

The doorframe, if it is painted at all, stands out against the facade and emphasizes the light or dark tones of the facade itself.

Aquitaine/Dordogne

Bourgogne / Côte-d'Or

Franche-Comté / Jura

Bourgogne / Yonne

Brittany / Morbihan / Île-aux-Moines

Brittany / Morbihan / Île-aux-Moines

Aquitaine/Dordogne

Centre/Indre-et-Loire

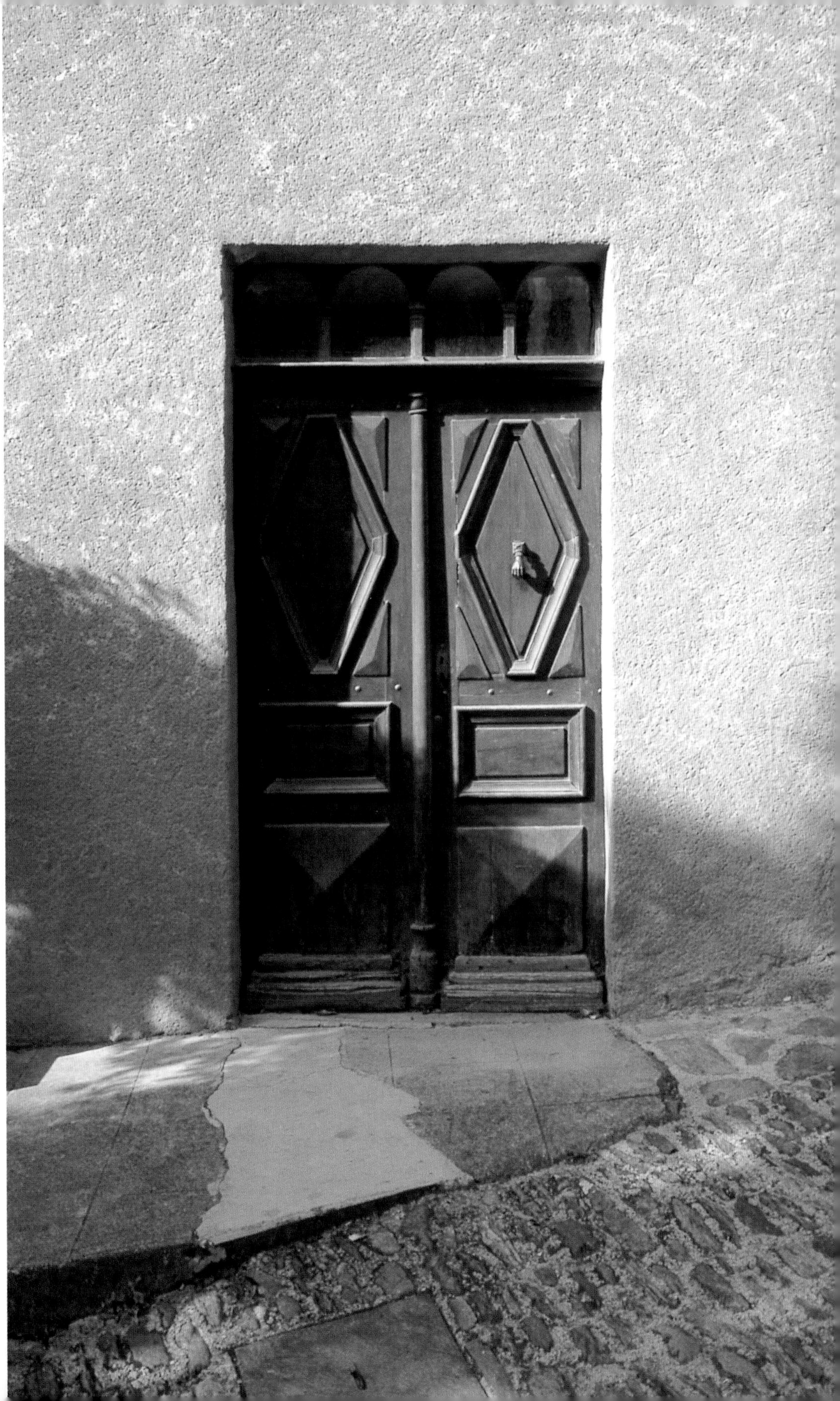

Ile-de-France/Seine-et-Marne

Aquitaine/Atlantic Pyrenees

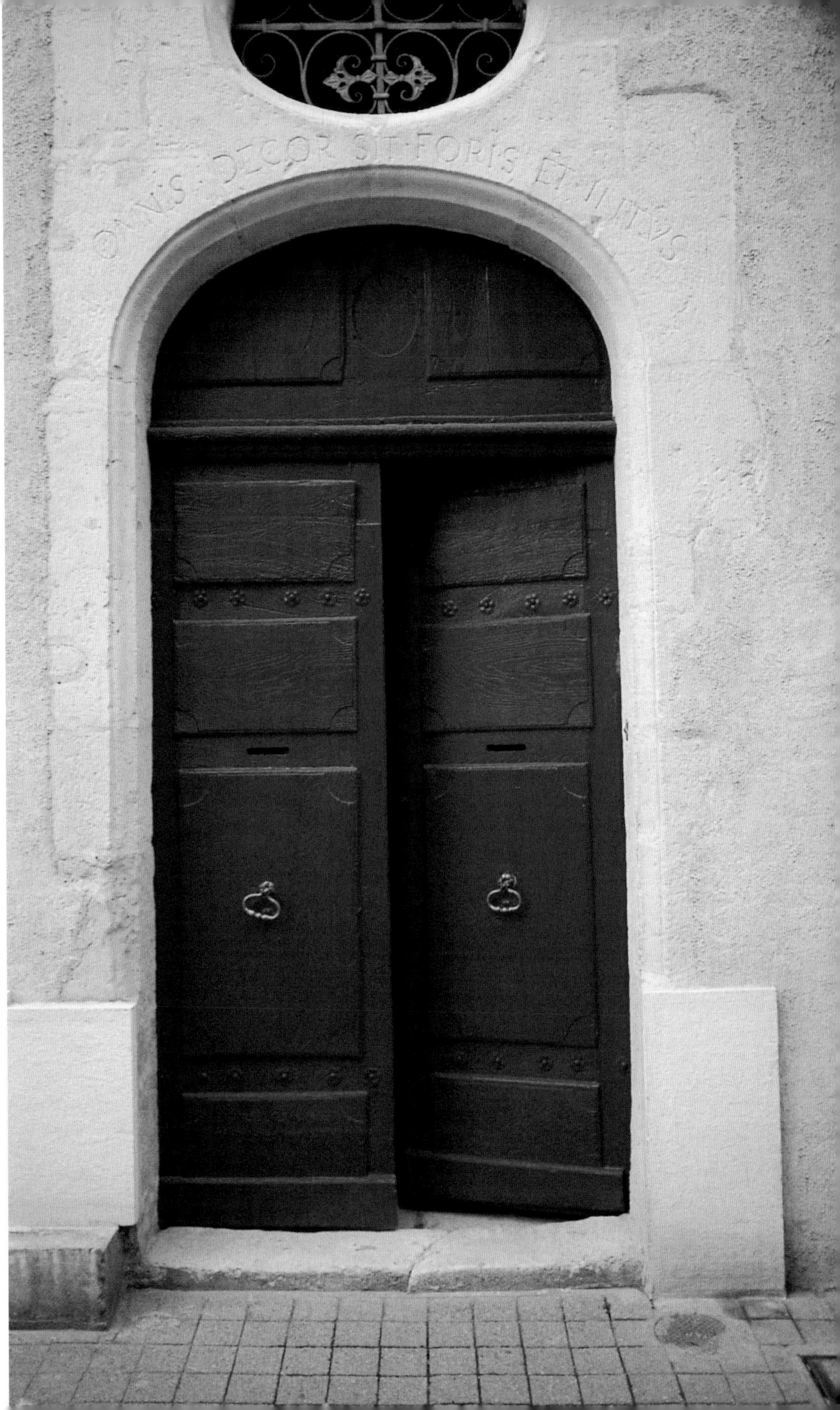

Limousin/Haute-Vienne/In summer

Limousin/Haute-Vienne/In autumn

Ile-de-France / Paris

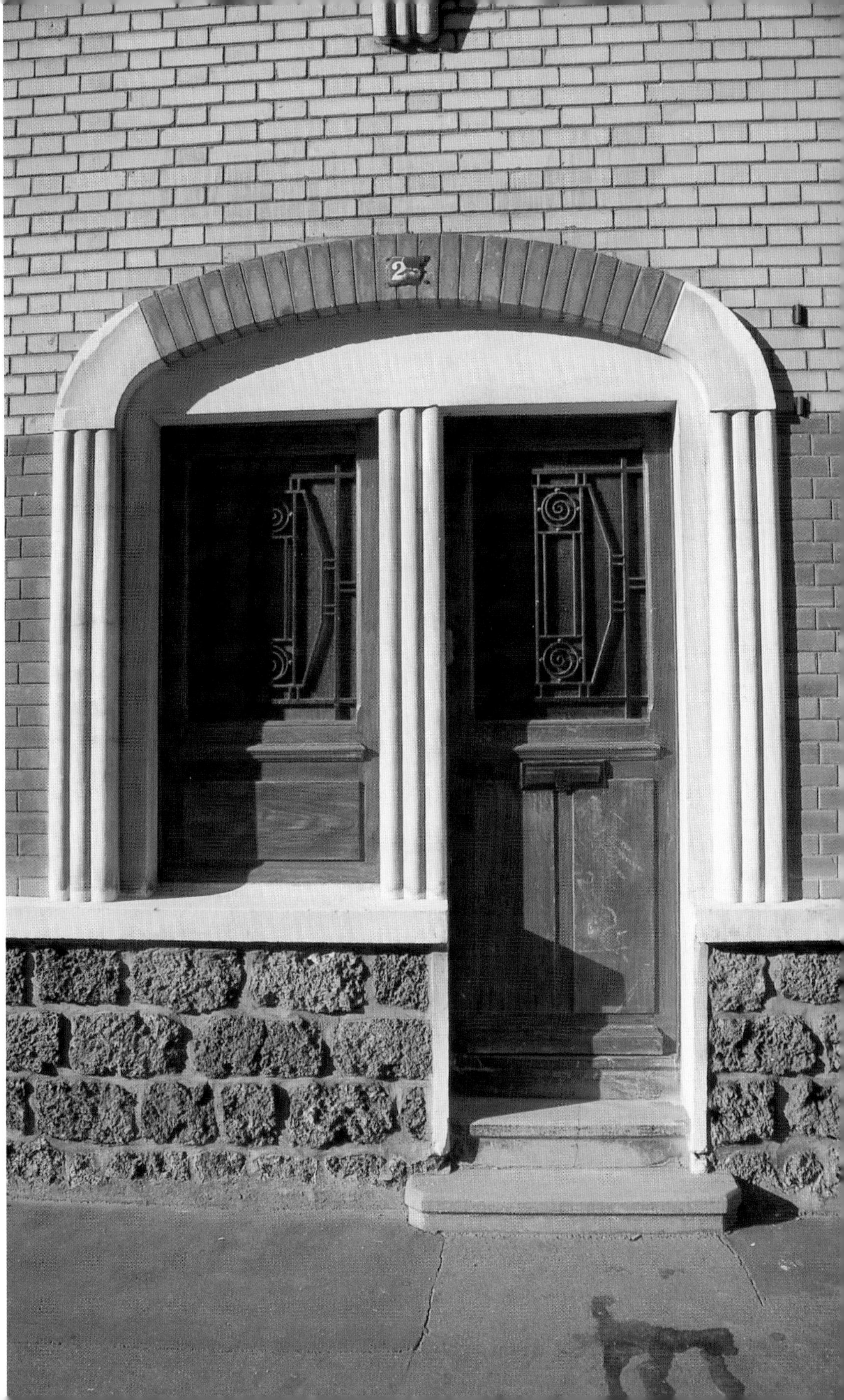
2

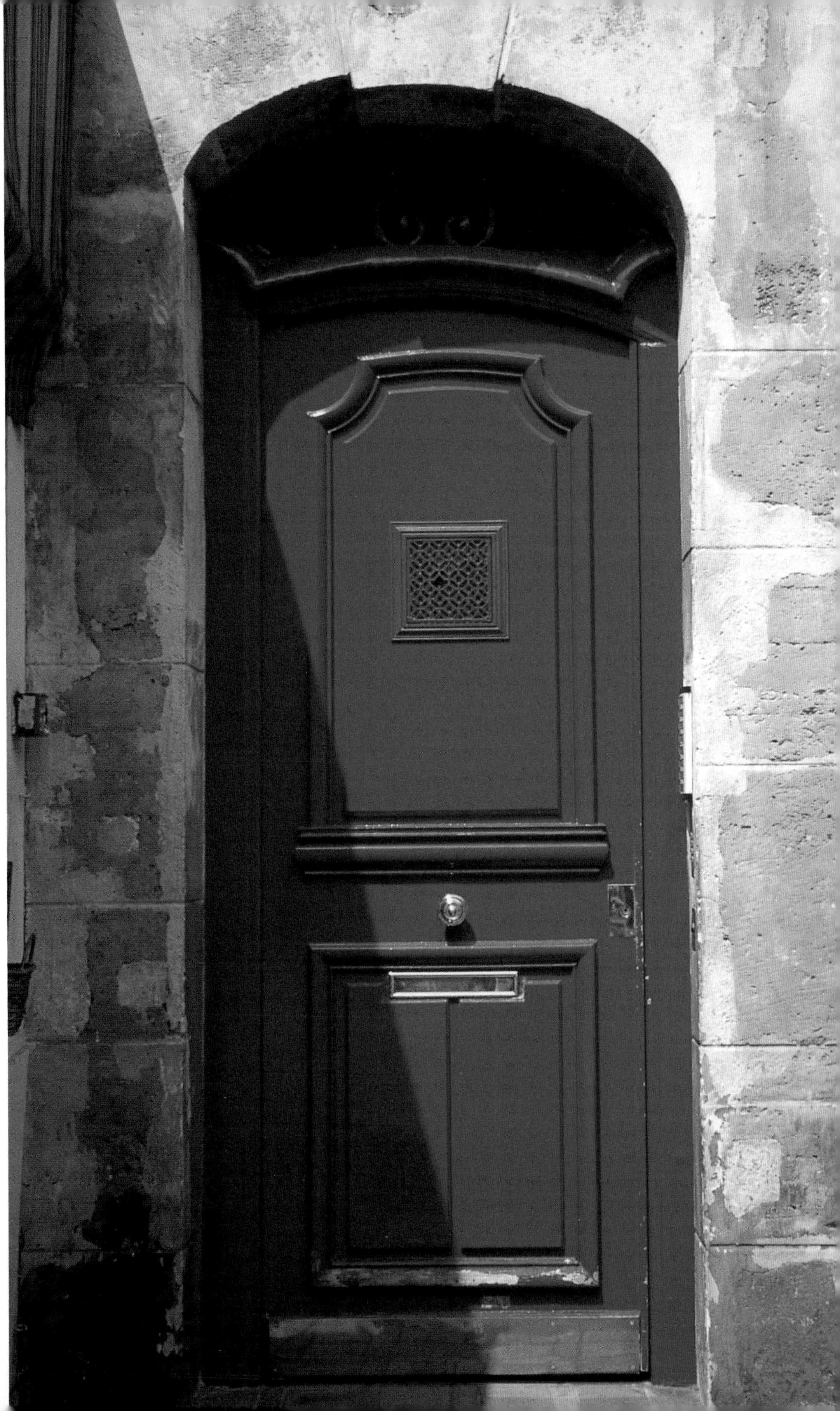

Ile-de-France/Paris

Europe

No matter what the style or period, the entrance of a home is an inescapable, privileged architectural element that offers itself up to whoever comes to polish its lacquered woodwork or brass doorknob.

Varying according to locale, the shape of the door—and even its materials and colors—can personalize the surface, thus bringing a sensitive dimension of emotion and symbolic value to the door. Indeed, the door, for both the visitor and the passerby, is a reflection of the tastes and personality of a home's residents, to the extent that they can express themselves in a defined context, within the traditions of their country or region. The geographical and cultural configuration of Europe allows for different typologies of doors according to construction techniques, doorway proportions, and frame type. Other significant elements such as bars, battens, molding, ironwork, ornament, and color serve to enrich the expressive character of this major facade element.

In Ireland and in Great Britain, the palette of colors used for the ensemble of door and frame constitutes the painted facade, on which lively, harmonious colors—and their resonating contrasts—can add a surprising touch. Opposing warm/cold, light/dark, and complementary colors are commonly used; for example, orange on a blue background, red on a black background, and frothy green on a yellow background.

In Scotland, the color of the door stands out strongly from its background thanks to a whitewash that enhances fieldstone door frames. The cutting of the woodwork is equally important: three vertical bars are assembled with three horizontal bars, forming a central, molded cross, thereby altering the look of the four dimpled panels, all of which is generally topped by a glass transom.

Color is again the agent that very decisively personalizes doorways in the Netherlands. The doors are covered by deep-toned lacquers, often a pure black, dark green, or a nearly black walnut stain. These decisive colors are emphasized by a door frame lacquered in bright white. This light/dark contrast gives woodwork a singular character that contrasts with the rough, structural material of the terracotta brick.

In Mediterranean countries, when the sun shines, the doors remain open to ensure interior ventilation throughout the home. A cotton or wooden-beaded curtain, or strips of cloth, serve as the door, thereby preserving the privacy of the home's occupants and protecting them from the sun's rays. The diversity of materials and colors of these curtains themselves are worth studying. In Toledo, the cloth is one color, often composed of subtle, earth-colored tones, sometimes olive or gray. However, in Burano, near Venice, the cloth is decorated in large, vertical bands of two different colors, white and blue, white and green, or white and red, and studded with printed floral motifs.

Belgium/Blankenberge

Belgium/Blankenberge

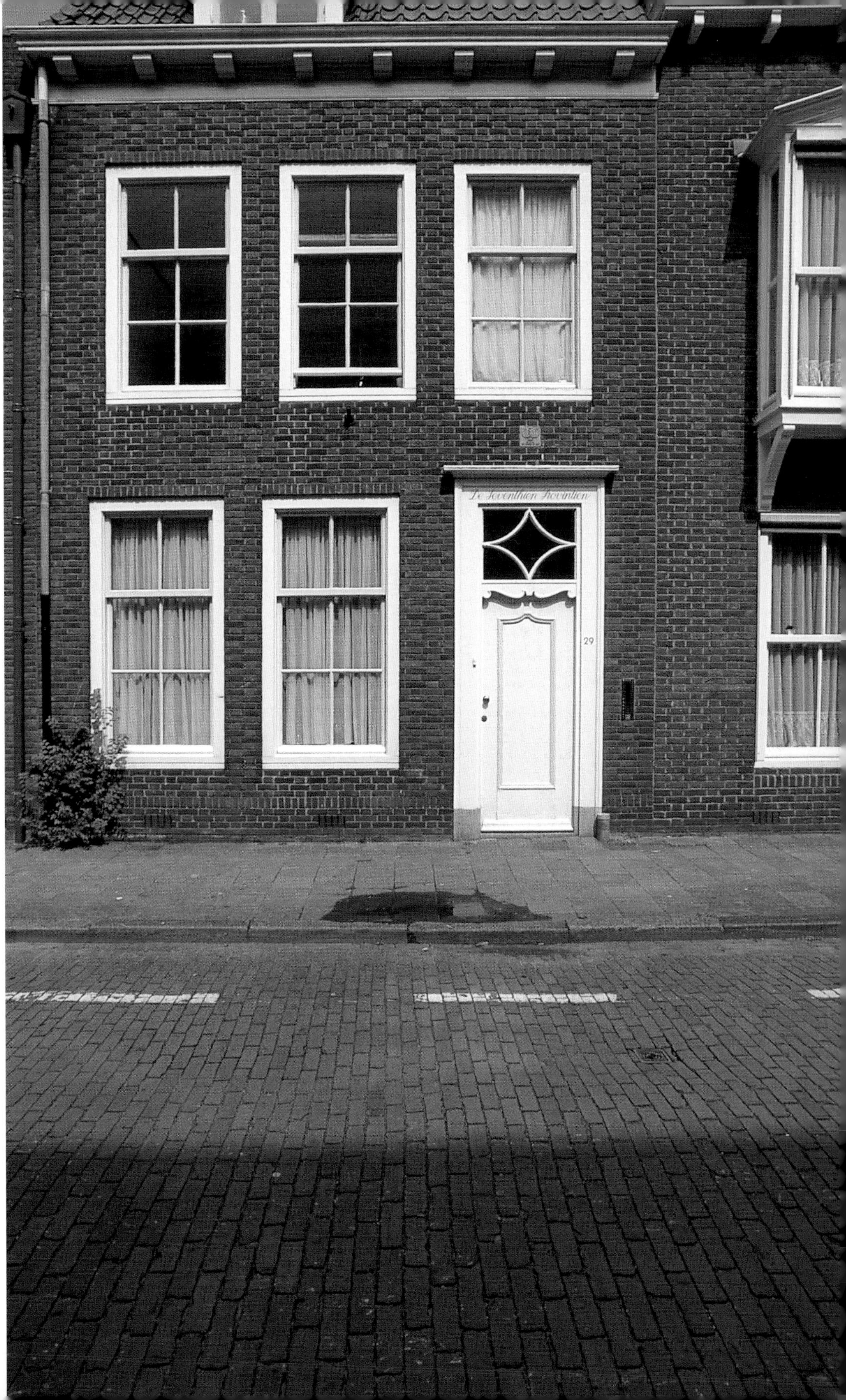
29

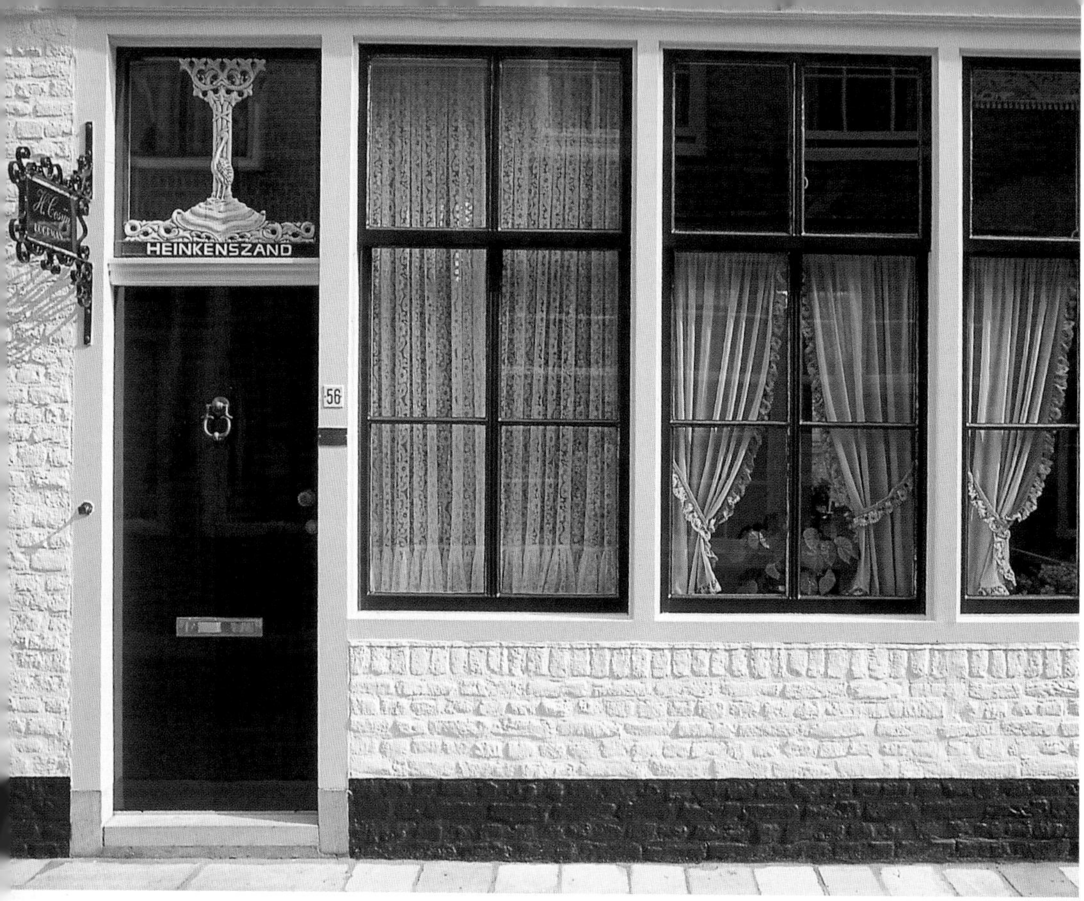

Netherlands/Middelburg

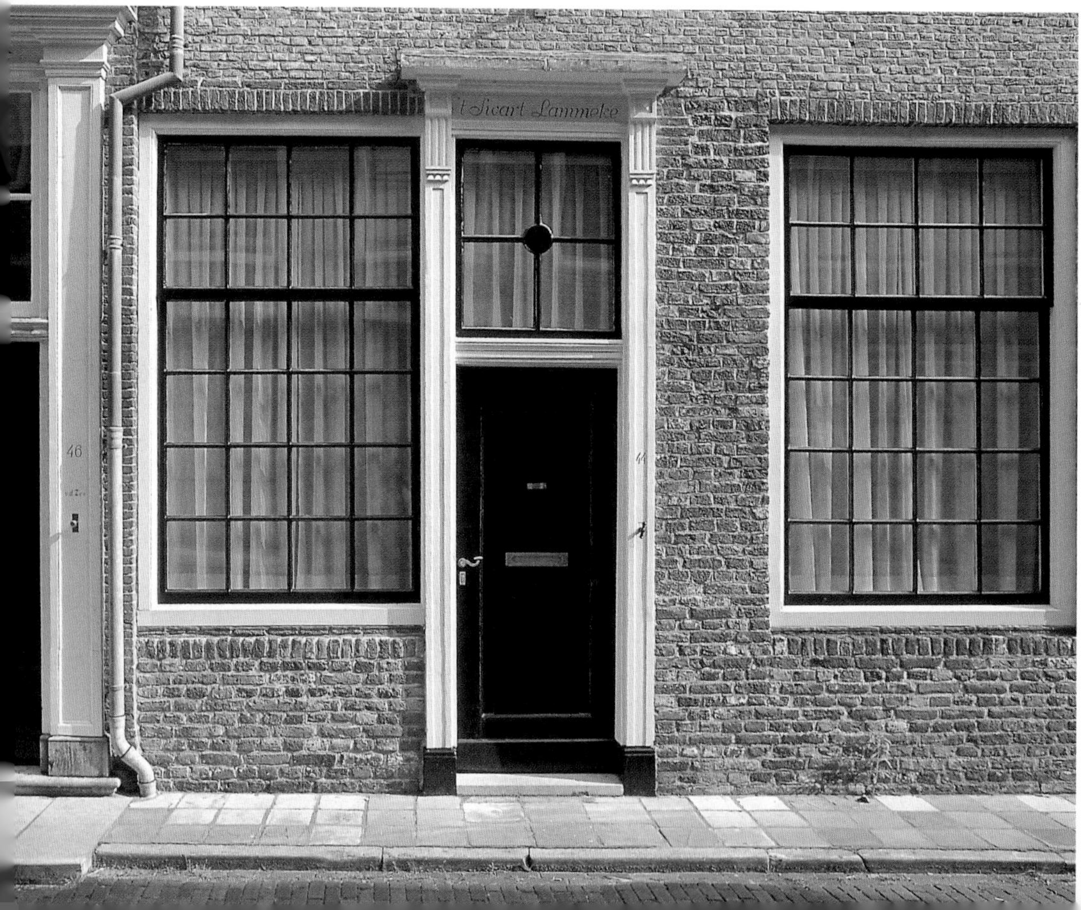

Netherlands/Middelburg

Denmark / Bornholm

Denmark/Bornholm

Scotland/Findochty

Scotland/Findochty

67

Ireland / Toormore

England/Bath

England / London

England/London

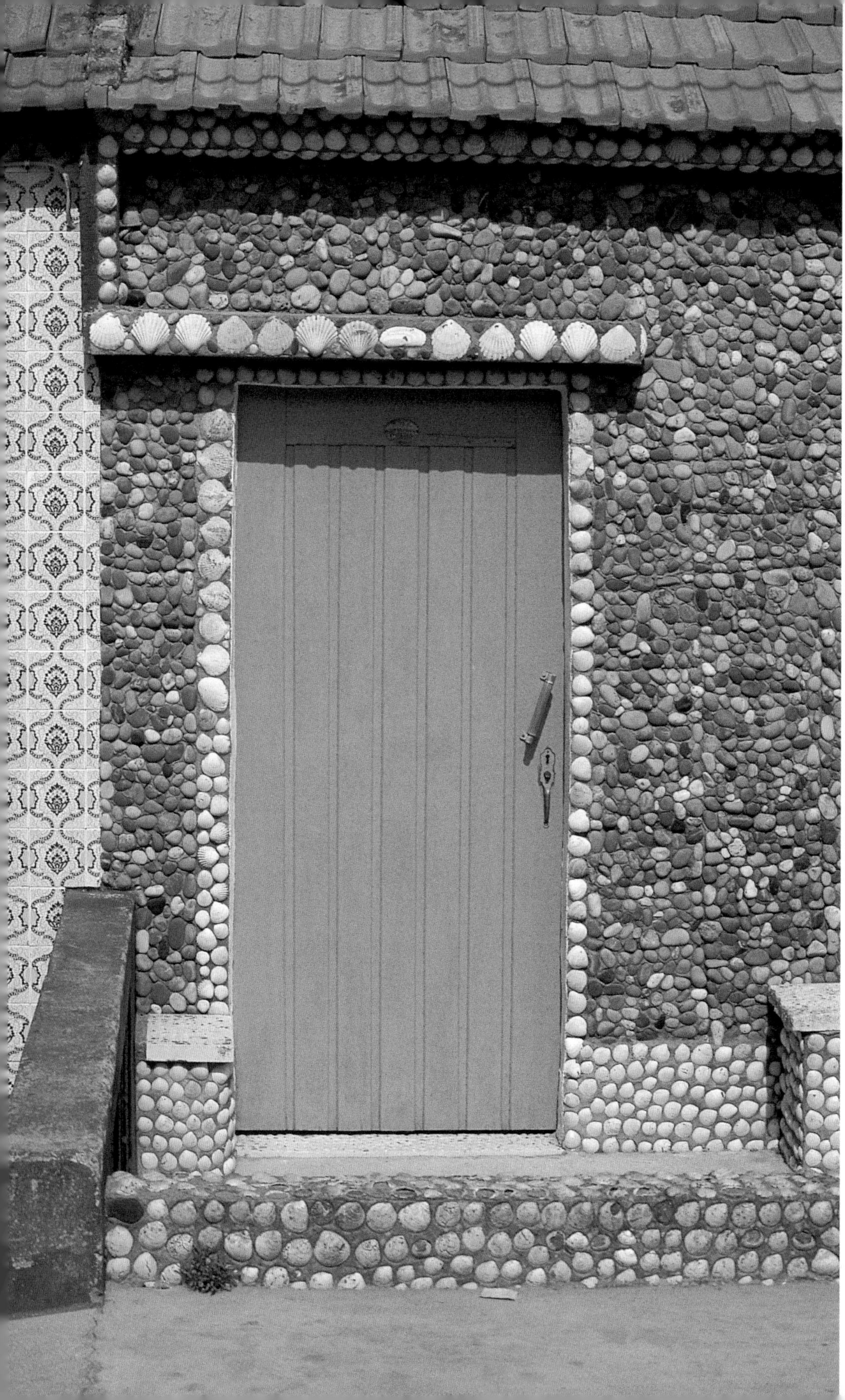

Portugal/Costa Nova

Portugal/Santa Luzia

Portugal/Faro

Portugal / Coimbra

150

Portugal / Costa Nova

Portugal/Costa Nova

Portugal / Costa Nova

Spain / New Castille / Consuegra

Spain / New Castille / Consuegra

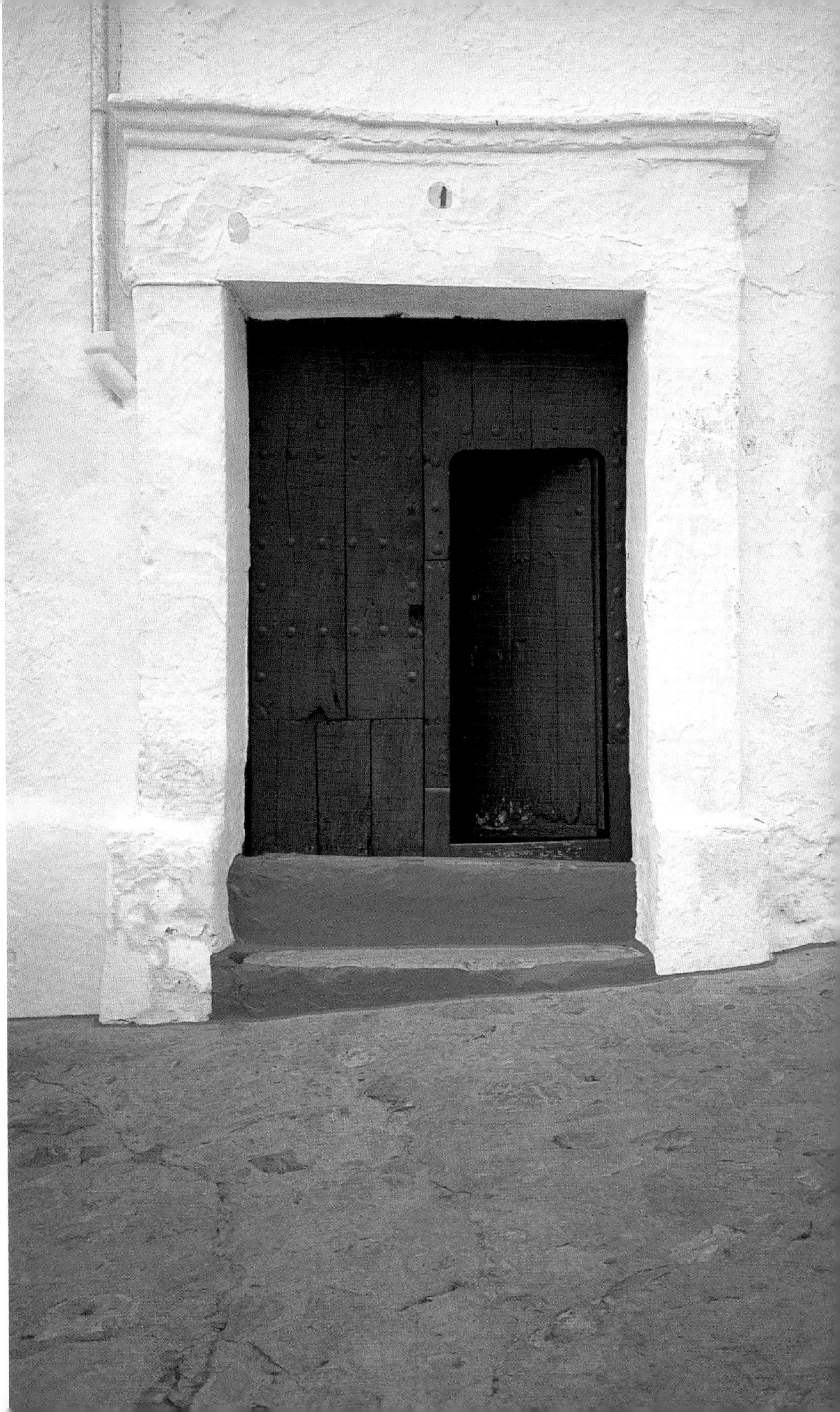

Spain/Andalusia/Grazalema

Italy/Burano

Italy/Procida

Greece / Karpathos / Olympia

Greece / Karpathos, Menetes

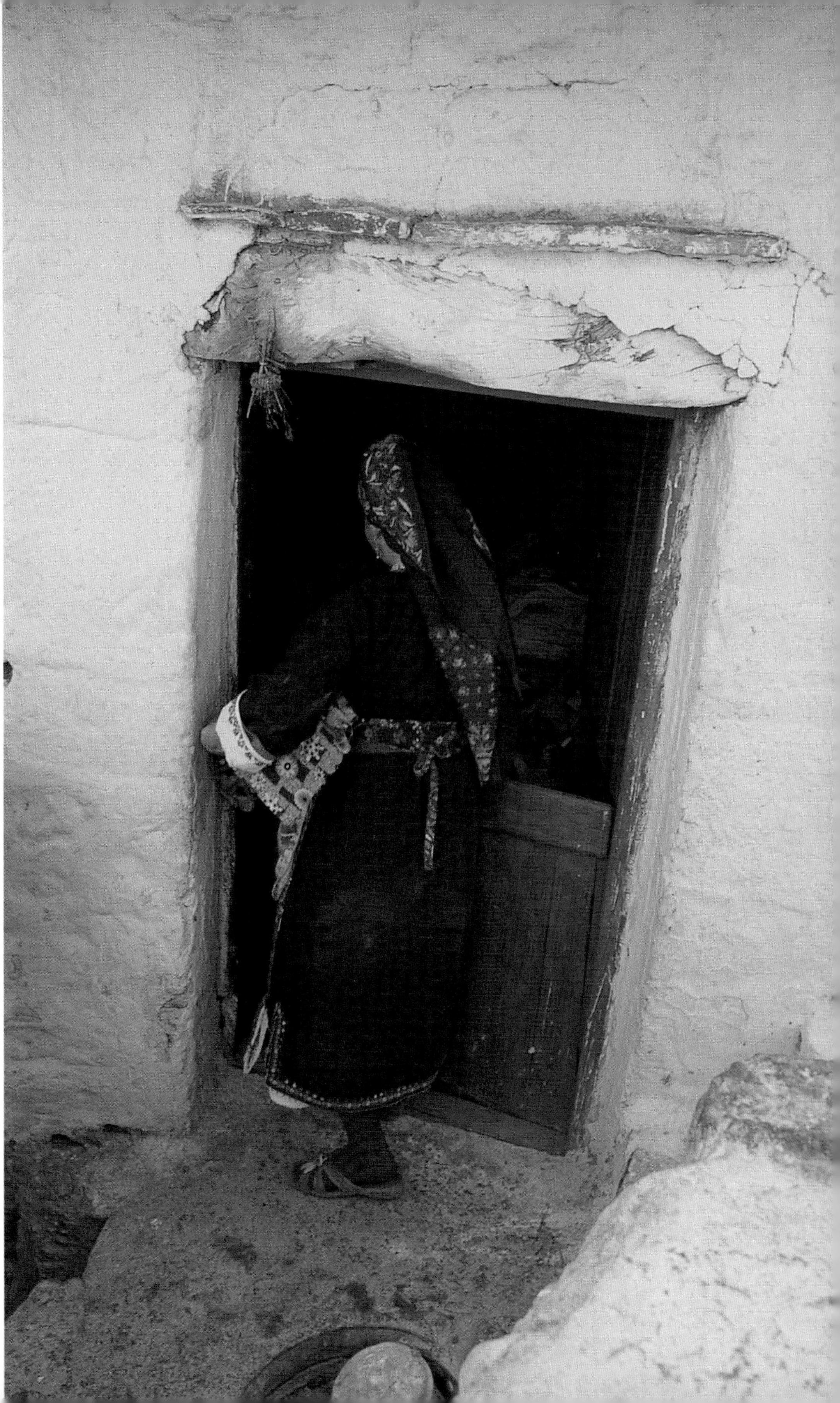

Greece/Karpathos/Olympia

Greece/Mykonos

Greece/Mykonos

Around the World

An inventory of doors is an invitation to travel and discover one of the most significant aspects of a place.

When you stop and ponder the traits that personalize the doors of one country or another, you assess the semantic and symbolic elements of the doors.

In Mozabite villages in southern Algeria, it is not unusual for the front of the door to be decorated with a crescent, the emblem of Islam, which may or may not be associated with the "hand of Fatima," an Arab talisman.

In China, during a marriage or the ceremony celebrating spring, two vertical banderoles made of red paper are attached to each side of the door; a poem written in black ink or in a golden ideogram expresses good wishes—happiness, a long life, and prosperity.

Feng shui, the Taoist art of living within an environment while recognizing its natural energies, considers the entrance of the home as its mouth. In effect, the door acts as a privileged bond between an enclosed environment that is necessary for health and wellness and the external natural resources that are indispensable to life and human relations.

In the Thar Desert in Rajasthan, where houses are made of adobe—the same color as their desert surroundings—the wives of camel herders decorate their whitewashed doorways with geometric motifs. These traditional ornaments, instituted to honor Lakshmi, the goddess of fortune and prosperity, signal the entryway of a home in a spectacular manner.

In Morocco, single or double doors made of sheet metal replace doors that were once made of wood. These modern doors are often decorated with pieces of flat iron shaped like native flowers or brightly colored diamonds, which are reminiscent of the geometric and polychromatic metalwork ornaments on Yemenite doors.

In Japan, sliding doors traditionally hide behind the *noren*, a two- or three-part curtain decorated with the family emblem, the *mon*, or with a corporate inscription, if the door in question is on a shop or workshop.

If the door itself and its frame are rich with meaning, looking attentively at the behavior of a home's inhabitants when they are about to pass through the doorway also allows a study of the habits and customs of the country. Here you can discover how the residents proceed through the door to announce their arrival, their attitude when the door opens, the exchanges of salutation on the doorstep, and the way in which the door is finally closed.

In North Yemen, where homes have four or five floors, visitors announce their arrival by means of a door knocker, and their host, after identifying them from the *mashrabiya* (screened bay window) in the upper levels where the living rooms are, opens the door using a cord that runs through all the floors and turns the latch. In South Yemen, the doorway is often hidden behind a screenlike wall; the space created between the two permits a woman to welcome her guests without being seen by passersby.

Clearly, the brief inventory we illustrate in this book concerns countries where craftwork, even today, is expressed in multiple, lively, and creative ways. Traditional techniques compete with more industrial techniques, rapidly leading to the creation of new materials and forms.

South Africa / Free State

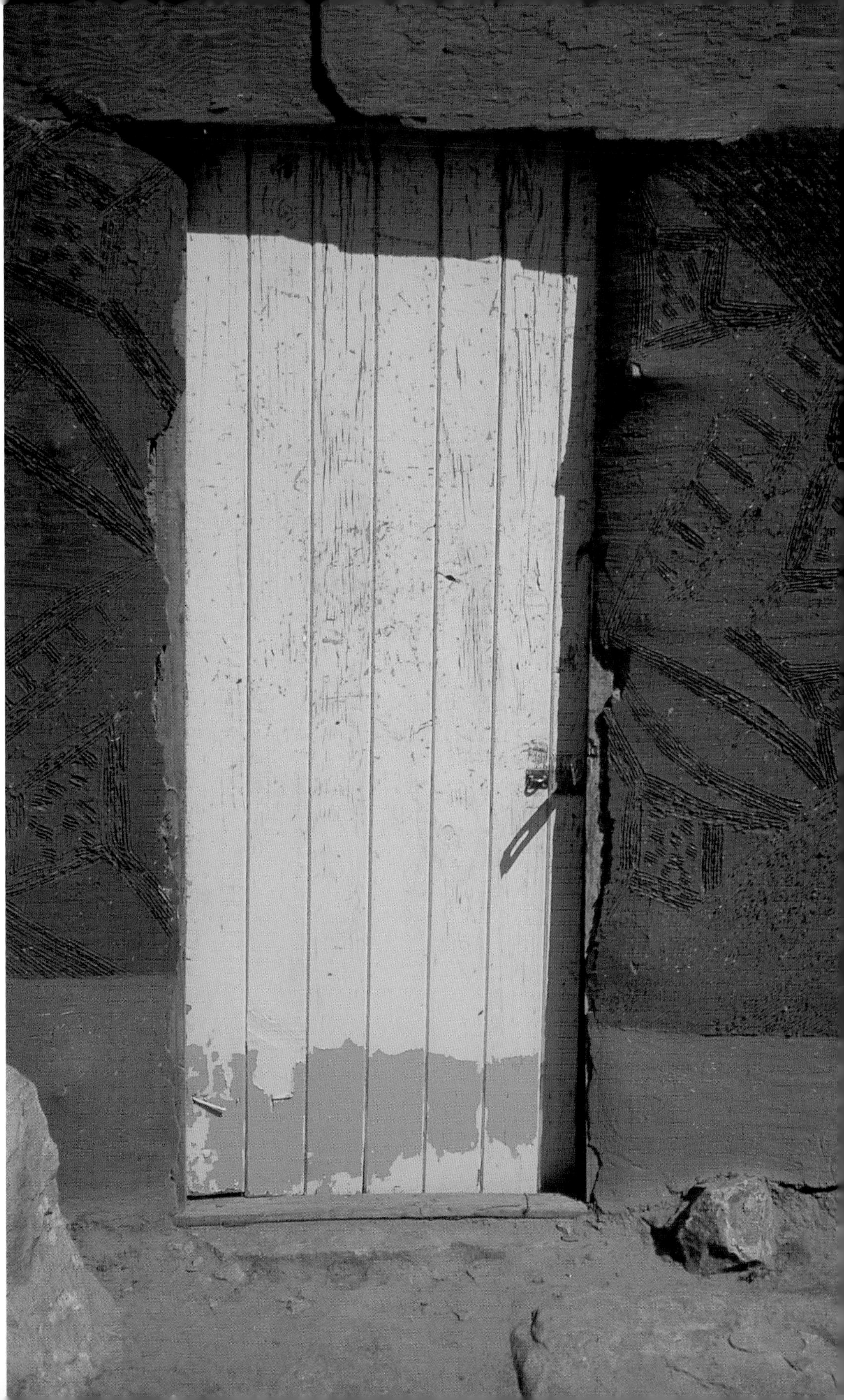

Algeria/Ghardaïa

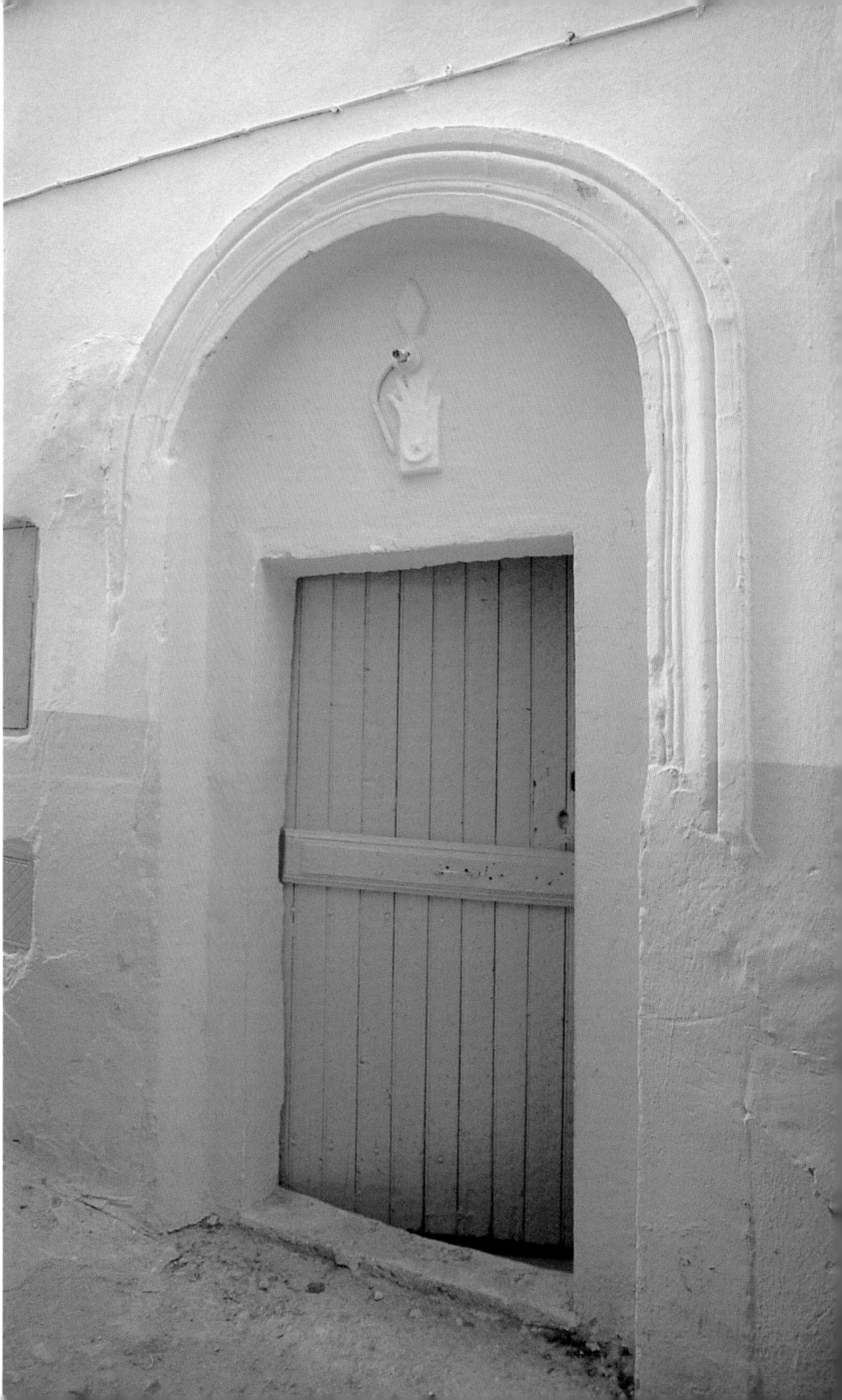

Algeria/Beni-Isguen

Algeria/Beni-Isguen

Morocco / Ouarzazate

Morocco / Ouarzazate

Morocco / Ouarzazate

Morocco / El-Kelaa-des-Mgouna

Tunisia/Sidi-Bou-Saïd

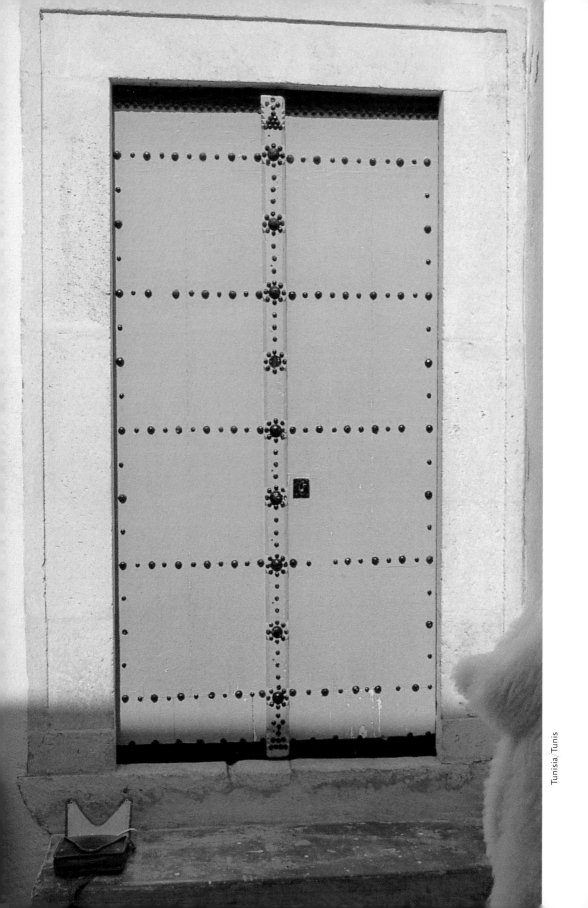

Tunisia, Tunis

Egypt / East Assouan

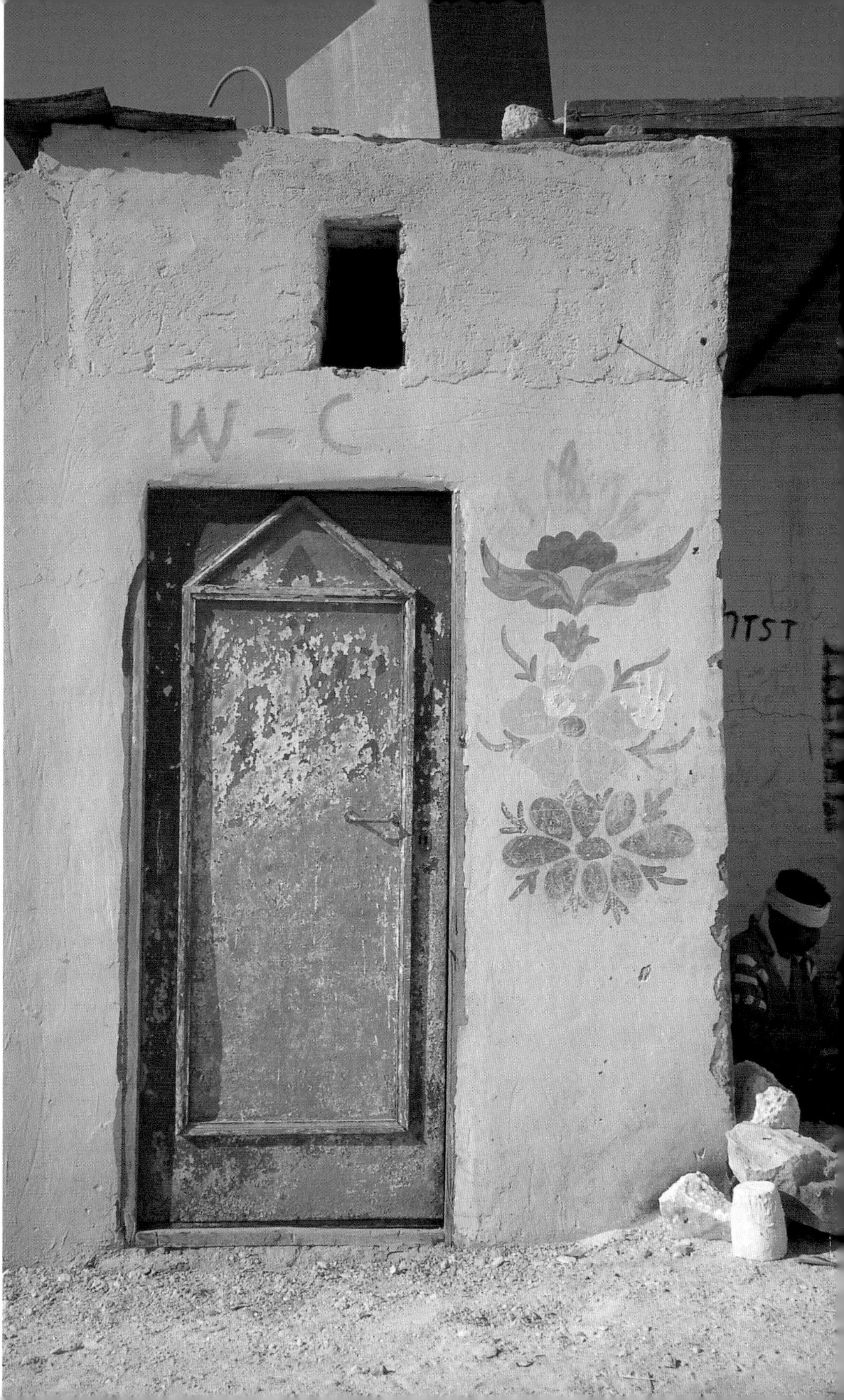
W-C

Egypt / East Assouan

Egypt / Luxor

Iran/Yazd

Iran/Ispahan

Iran/Yazd

South Yemen / Tarim

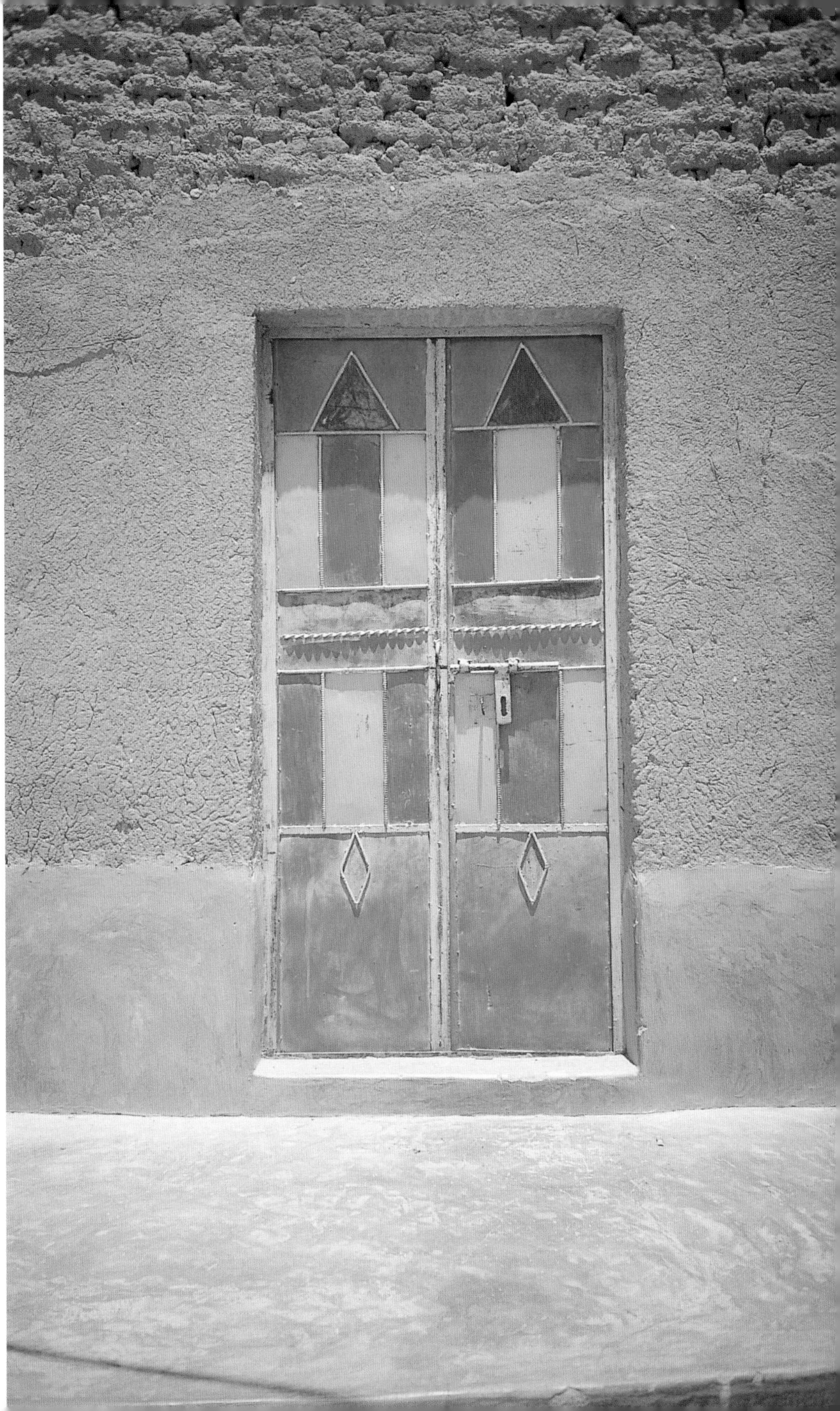

South Yemen/Tarim

North Yemen / Sanaa

South Yemen / Tarim

South Yemen/Tarim

South Yemen/Shibam

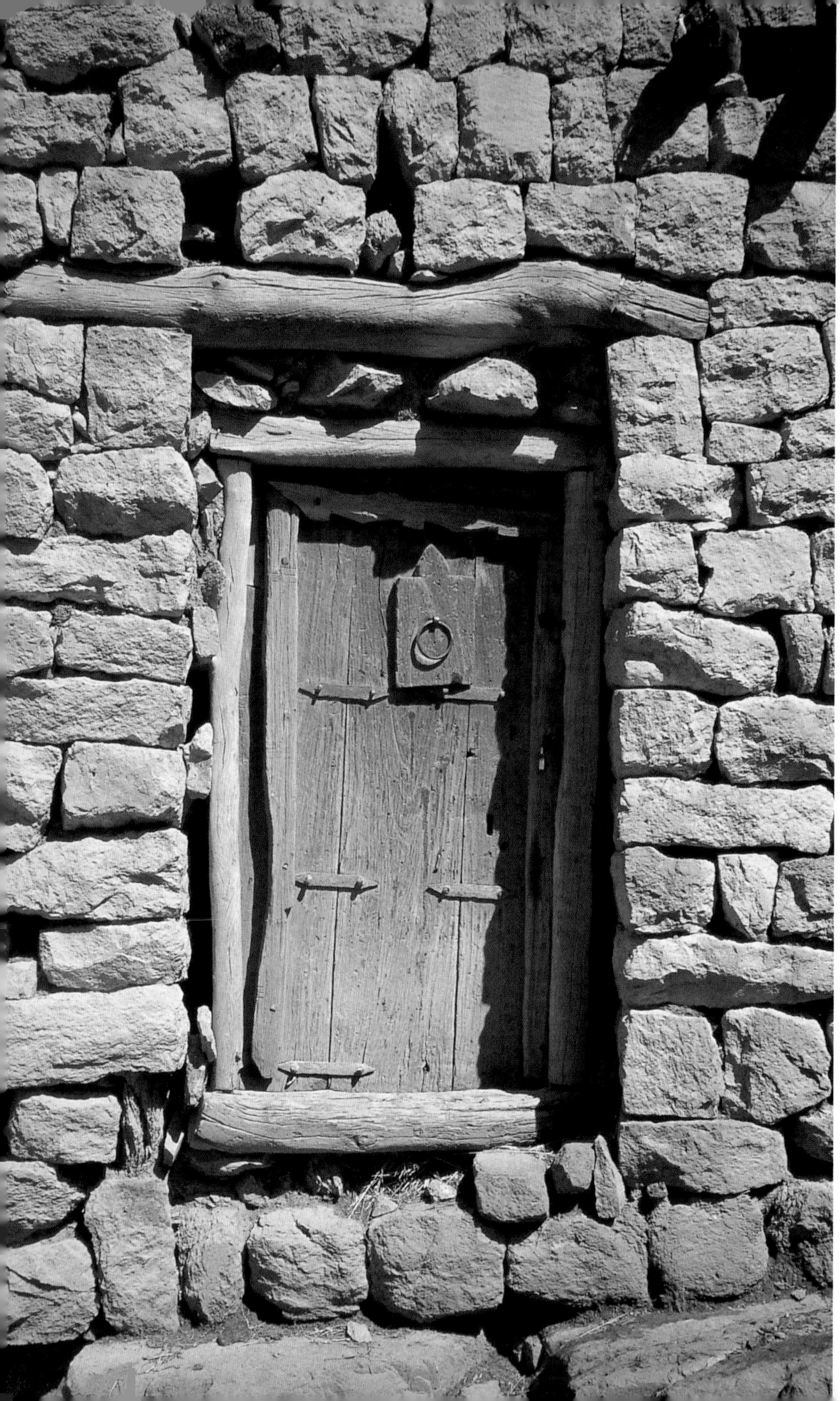

North Yemen/Al-Hajjara

India/Rajasthan/Jodhpur

India/Rajasthan/Jodhpur

India/Rajasthan/Jodhpur

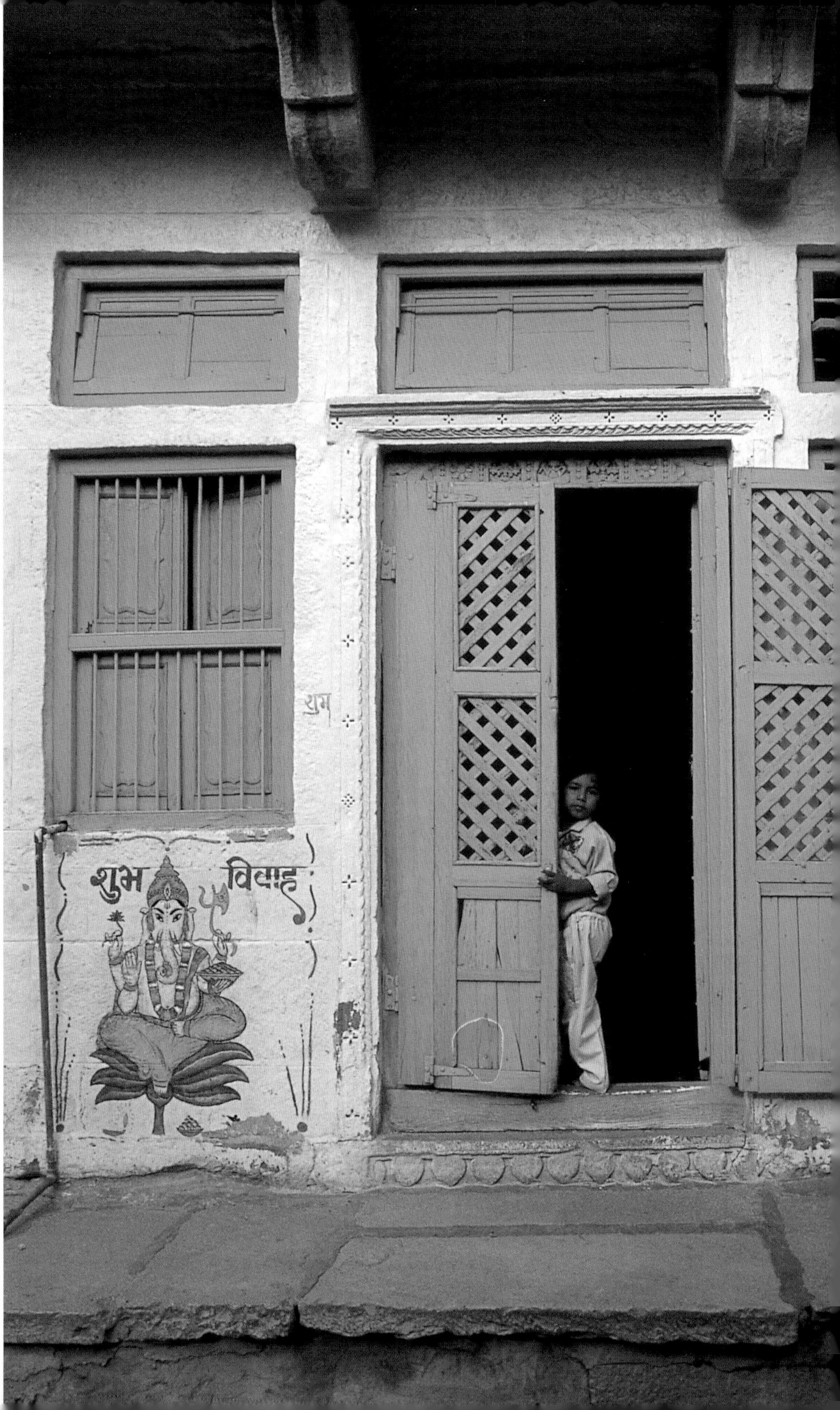
शुभ
शुभ विवाह

India/Rajasthan/Jaisalmer

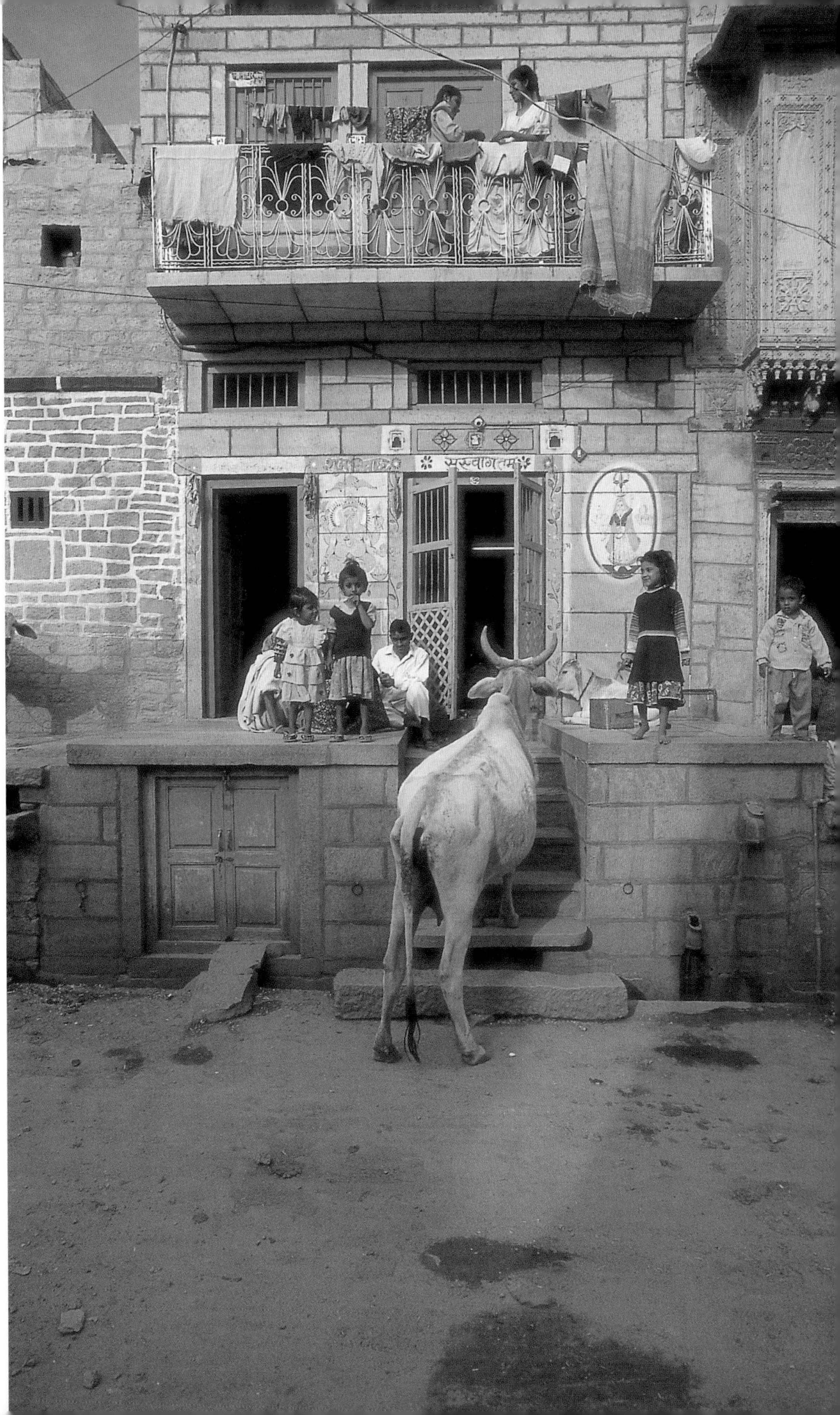

India / Rajasthan / Jaipur

India / Rajasthan / Jaisalmer

India / Rajasthan / Thar Desert

China/Han Hui Province/Wang Zhai

China / Han Hui Province / Wang Zhai

China,/Han Hui Province,/Wang Zhai

China/Shanghai

China/Shanghai

Japan/Kyoto (Inari Jinja)

Japan/Kyoto

Japan/Kyoto

Brazil/Salvador de Bahia

Brazil/Pernambuco/Sabara

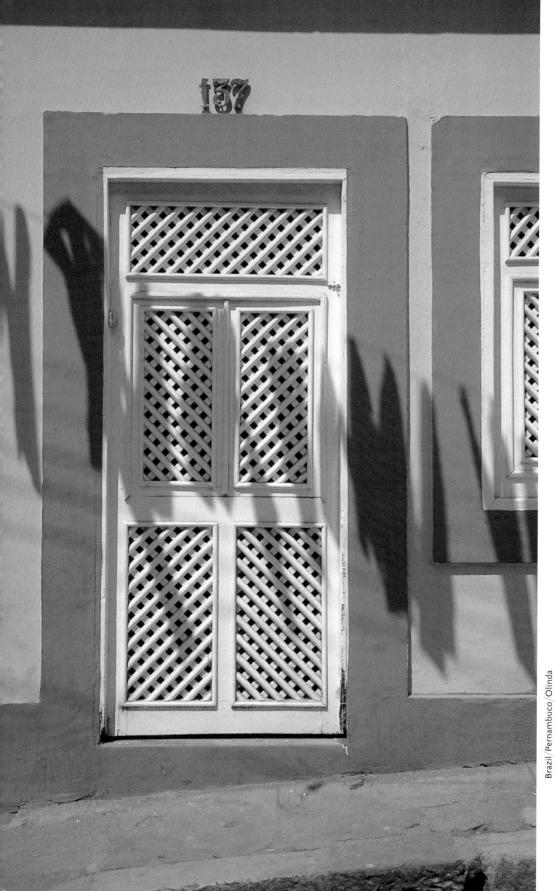

Brazil/Pernambuco/Olinda

Brazil/Pernambuco/Santa Amaro

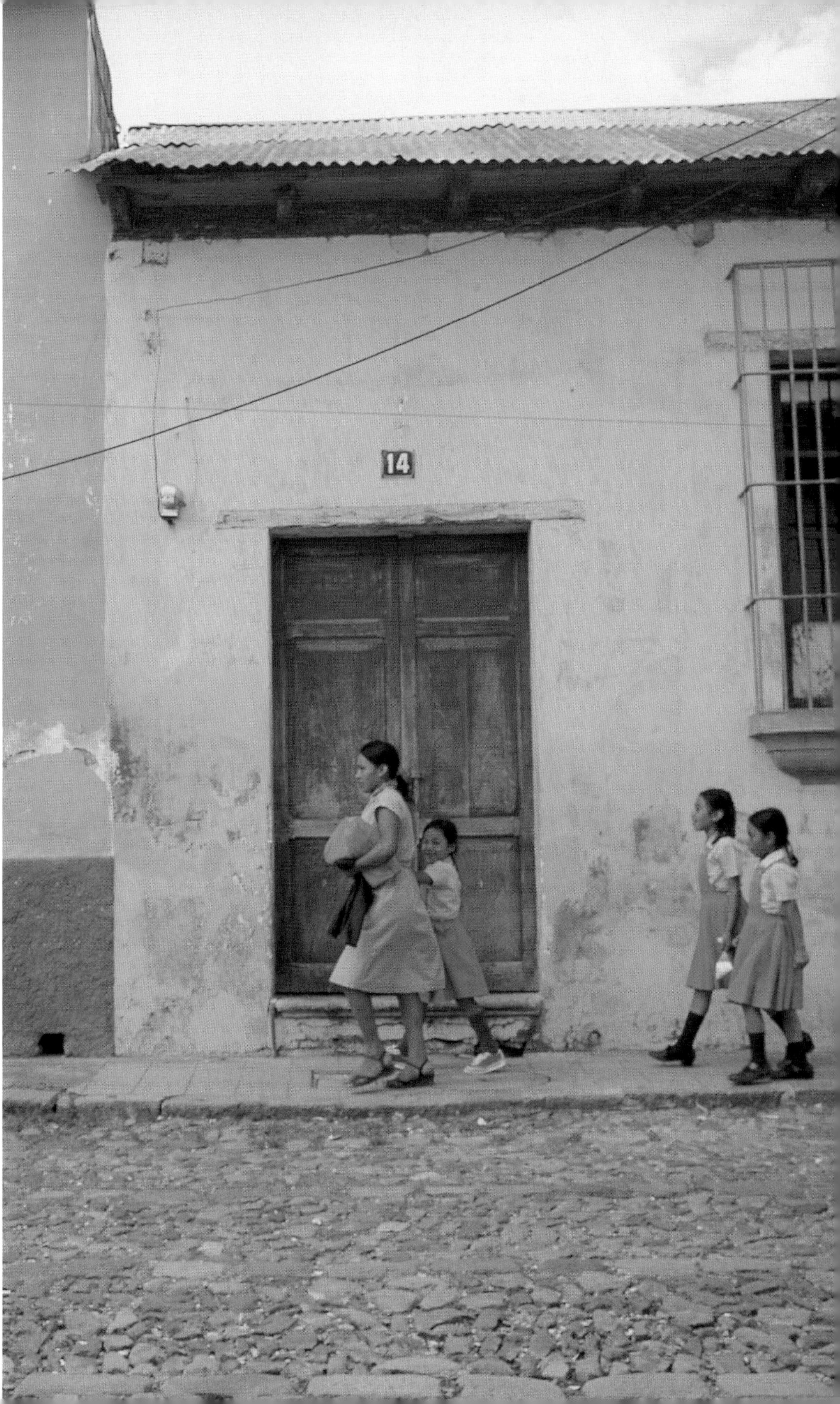

Guatemala/Antigua

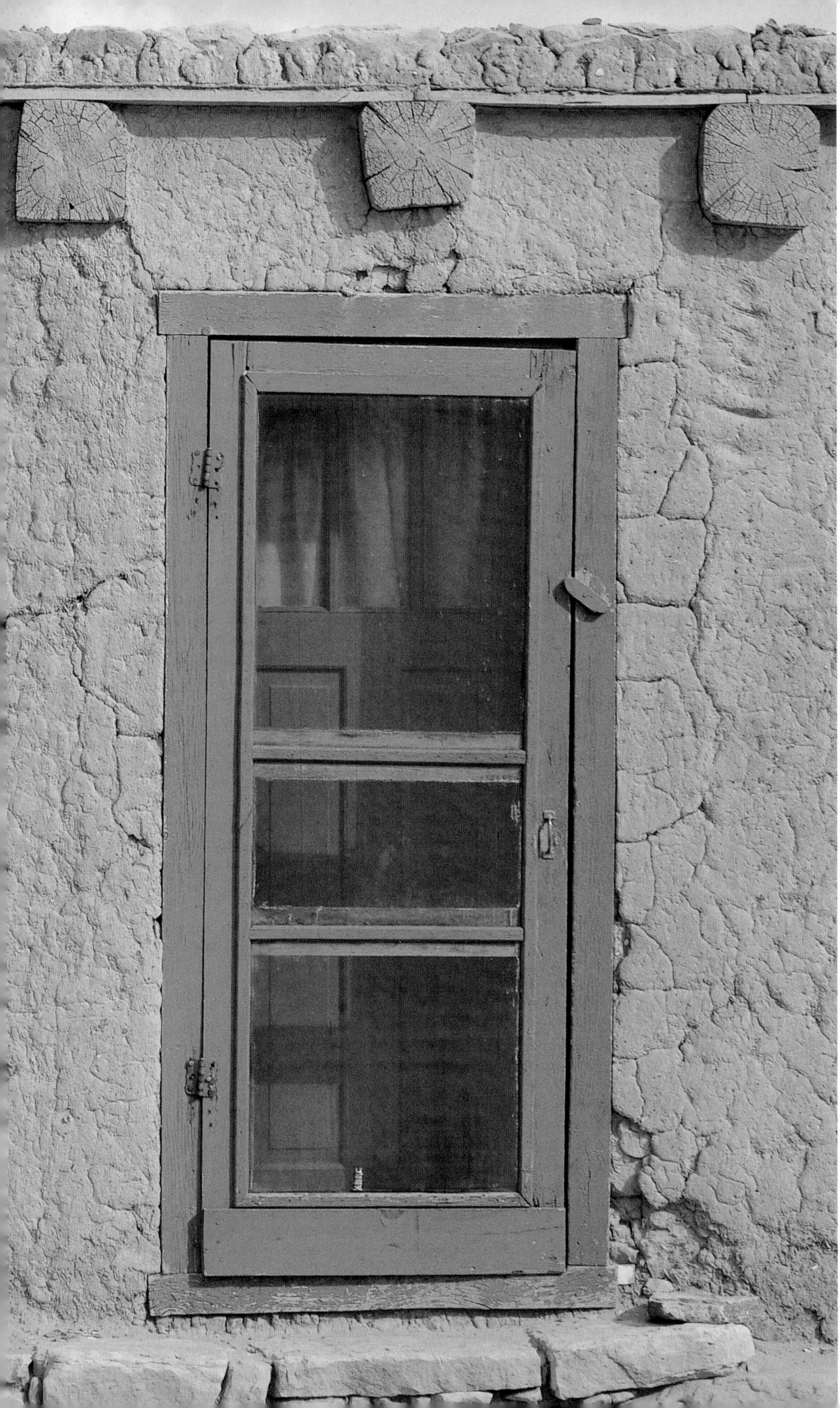

United States / New Mexico / Acoma

United States/New Mexico/Acoma

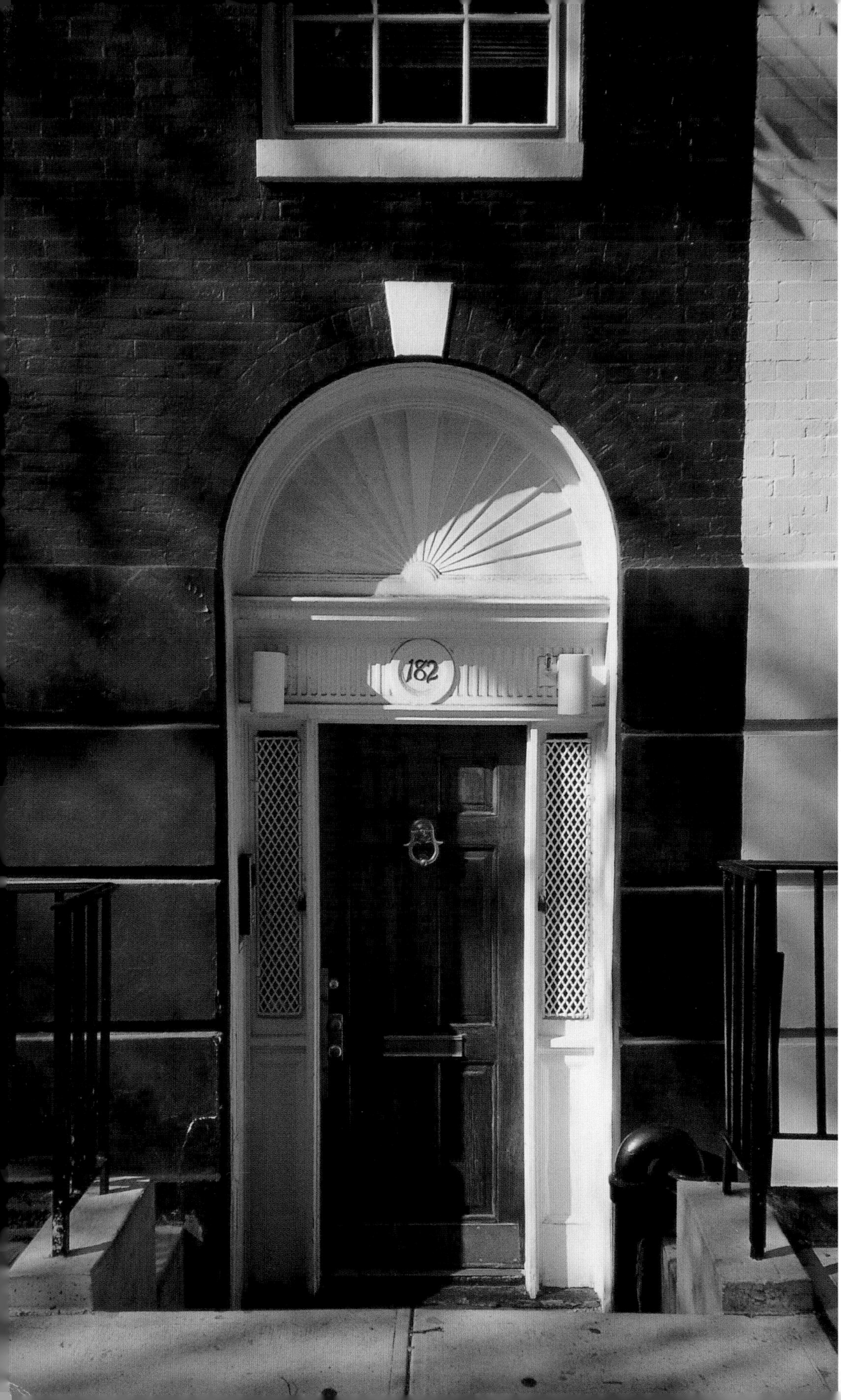

United States/New York/Greenwich Village

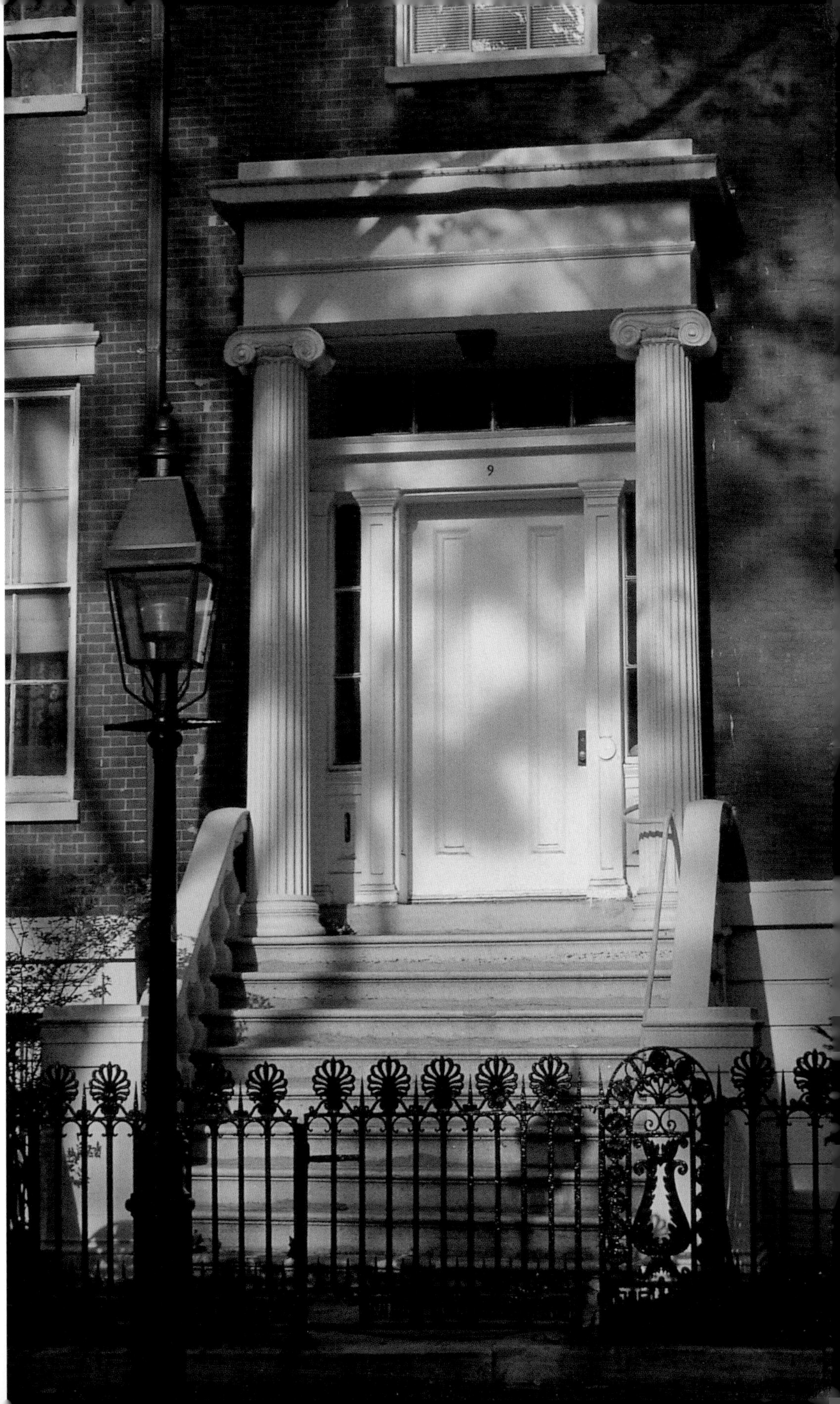
9

Credits